THE FIRE

MY COLLECTION OF POEMS AND SHORT STORIES

AISHWARYA JATHISH

Dedicated to the writing potential in me..............

Contents

Foreword

The poems are about life, childhood,solitude,christmas,and about my mother who has loved me more than herslef.This book os dedicated to her as well and the final poem is also about her.Please read this if you like it and generate writing potential in you too.......

Preface

The contents in this book are poems are about life, childhood,solitude,christmas,and about my mother who has loved me more than herslef.This book os dedicated to her as well and the final poem is also about her.Please read this if you like it and generate writing potential in you too.......

Acknowledgements

I have written this book my myself but I thank my family for their co-operation and notionpress.com for helping me publish this e-book.

Prologue

The poems are about life, childhood,solitude,christmas,and about my mother who has loved me more than herslef.This book os dedicated to her as well and the final poem is also about her.Please read this if you like it and generate writing potential in you too.......

1. LIFE

Life is a mixture of joy and sorrows,
One has to push it like a wheel barrow,
It does not depend on how you live,
But in your life what you give.
Pain ,joy ,anger and grief,
Does not matter as our life is brief,
What does matter is how much you gave,
To others and how you behave.
Life has neither past, present or future,
It is as still and stable as the nature,
Life is just a series of events,
That passes as quickly as water currents.
People you see new and today,
Won't be there with us everyday,
So, learn to share, help, forgive and forget,
And do not care about the return you will get.
Life depends on what you do,
Life is sweet and lovely too,
Life depends on how you live,
And also mainly on how much you give.

2. SOLITUDE

I once went to a jungle,
Where, like how the bells jingle,
The clinging of the branches were heard,
And I thought it was the sound of the sheep's herd.
Then, when I came to know,
That the wood was too scary for now,
I slowly walked through the solitude,
And then I was filled with gratitude.
Gratitude towards the birds that chirp,
Gratitude towards that solitude,
Gratitude towards the leaves that slip,
From my hands which were rude.
Solitude and Gratitude,
Both have a relation that's cool,
Solitude changes your attitude,
It makes you as chill as a pool.
Then, came the creatures grateful,
Though some were so powerful,
Grateful toward that solitude,
Grateful towards that shady-wood.
There were birds chirping,
There were buds blooming,
There was the greatest gift one could get,
For there was solitude leading to peace and rest.

3. AN ODE TO CHRISTMAS

Oh! My gentle snow,
I wonder if you did know,
How the winter brings joy,
For it brings Christmas which we enjoy.
Oh! My sweet tinkling bells,
I wonder if you would tell,
That Christmas is so much fun,
For that's when the children do merrily run.
Oh! My Santa Claus,
I wonder if you could close,
The doors and windows of the houses,
After filling it with surprises.
Oh! My Christmas cap,
You lean at the top like a tap,
Your red colour of roses,
Remind people of the wish they chooses.
Oh! My Christmas tree,
You look as if filled with glee,
For it is the season of joy and gifts,
And also the time of the birth of the Christ.

4. FRIENDS

Lost in the world of past,

I did search them everywhere,

I felt I was lonely and lost,

For where they were ; I wasn't aware.

I cried till my tears blinded me,

But, they just did not come back,

In the hope that they would come to me,

I was on my bed-lying with the support of my back.

When no-one finally came,

I did go wild,

But, I myself did tame,

Those stupid, angry , feelings.

Now I'm very much sure,

That they will never come back,

But, still my heart in friendship so pure,

Cannot just bear being alone in the shack.

Finally, I wished them all the best,

With all my love and heart,

So that my soul may, for sometime rest,

And stop thinking for a big, big, heart,

And that I would rather become still like a stuck chart.

5. WHEN HE CAME DOWN TO EARTH

When he came down to Earth,
Lighting the fire of the hearth,
He brought the gift of joy ,
Which people did enjoy
.When he came down to Earth,
Lighting the fire of the hearth,
He brought the dove of peace,
For orelse, the world would freeze
.When he came down to Earth,
Lighting the fire of the hearth,
He brought the air of kindness,
Which took away the world's blindness.
When he came down to Earth,
Lighting the fire of the hearth,
He brought the warmth of love,
Which shone in the world like a white-glove.
When he came down to Earth,
Lighting the fire of the hearth ,
He gave us the heavenly blessings,
Which made our lives interesting.

My Poems

My poems are both happy and melancholic, funny and devotional , spiritual and moral as well as romantic which here means being close to nature's beauty. Please read them, get those feelings in you, and become a writer as feelings are what makes one a writer.